A Plea For Ragged Schools, Or, Prevention Better Than´ Cure: Supplement To "a Plea For Ragged Schools."

Thomas Guthrie

SUPPLEMENT

TO

"A PLEA FOR RAGGED SCHOOLS."

BY THE

REV. THOMAS GUTHRIE.

SECOND EDITION.

EDINBURGH:

JOHN ELDER, 139, PRINCE'S STREET.

WILLIAM COLLINS, GLASGOW; AND JAMES NISBET & CO. LONDON.

———

MDCCCXLVII.

EDINBURGH : PRINTED BY MILLER AND FAIRLY.

SUPPLEMENT, &c.

THE "Plea" fell much like a small spark among combustibles, calling forth, what had previously existed in the public mind,—a very lively and general interest in the welfare of the outcast children of society. For some time after its first publication, every day brought letters expressive of sympathy, and offering co-operation; and men so responded to the call, as to manifest impatience for the organization of a scheme, and a public meeting at which it might be launched. Such a meeting, patronised by gentlemen of all ranks and denominations, was at length held : our scheme was launched amid the plaudits of a concourse of spectators; and while many watched its progress and blessed it with their prayers, off it went to save the castaways. We built our scheme after the model of those in Aberdeen and Dundee. So far as we knew, they had been in all respects universally approved of. Men in office and men of literature, the friends of philanthropy and the advocates of education, had pronounced on these schools an unqualified encomium; while the power of these schools to accomplish the object in view was, as Dr Chalmers used to say of other things, a matter, not of experiment, but of experience. We had ample and most satisfactory details of the School in Aberdeen; we had visited the School in Dundee; and having told what our eyes had seen and our ears had heard, it was unanimously carried, without a

murmur of disapprobation, far less one clear dissenting voice,
that our School should be, in the main, modelled after the fashion
of these. This accordingly was done; and at the close of this
"Supplement," the reader will find the Rules and Constitution
of our Edinburgh School, as proposed by the Committee, and
unanimously adopted by a large meeting of the citizens. For
some short while matters went smoothly enough: there was
confidence within our Committee, and no cloud without; and
the happy, I will say the holy, spectacle was seen, of men who
had been at war now cultivating the arts of peace, forgetting
differences in a common object, and met with swords turned
into ploughshares, to break up the ground which had long lain
fallow.

At first we did not attempt much. There was great difficulty
found in procuring suitable accommodation for the Schools in
the central part of the city.* Besides, the objects of our charity, being strangers to subordination, had to be disciplined
and broken in; and there could not be a greater mistake, or
a grosser misrepresentation, than to allege, as was done, that
the small number of our scholars was owing to any aversion
which the Roman Catholics felt to participate in the benefits of
our School. I was warned against sweeping in an unmanage-
able number at first, by a circumstance which I heard, when
Lord Ashley did me the honour to take me to one of the Ragged
Schools in London. The School we visited was in Westmin-
ster, and the building where they assembled had a remarkable
history. Some time before it was turned to its present purpose, this building had been used as a tavern, and was resorted
to by the thieves of that district of the city as their favourite
rendezvous. There they met to plan, and from thence they went
forth to execute, their deeds of crime. Even then they had a
Sabbath school in it; but what a school! Then the large room

---

* This difficulty has been in a great measure removed through the kindness
of the Rev. Mr Smith and the Kirk-session of the Tolbooth parish, who have
in the meantime accommodated us with a large and commodious school-room
at Ramsay Garden, Castlehill.

in which I stood was filled with the ruffians and robbers of the neighbourhood. At one end the younger thieves,—those who were in training,—pursued the art of pocket-picking. If the lesson was not well performed, the bungler was apprehended and dragged by a sham policeman to the other end of the room. There, caricaturing a court of justice, sat a presiding ruffian, dressed out in the wig, and gown, and garb of a Judge, by whom, amid all the formalities of the law, the culprit was tried, and, in the course of this mock assize, was taught how to fence and evade,—where to be silent, and how to speak,—when, in his future career of guilt and crime, this farce had passed into a dreadful tragedy. And now, beneath that very roof where unhappy outcasts had been trained in wickedness and sin, a Ragged School presents a very different scene,—provides a very different teaching. We found a Ragged School there in admirable order, filled with the very objects of such a charity, and, among others, we remember two. A boy was pointed out to us, whose bed, the preceding winter, had been the hollow of the iron roller in one of the parks: the other had been brought to the school by one of the most notorious thieves in the neighbourhood, who implored them to receive the child as the only means of saving him from ruin; adding, when his strange request was granted, as he looked round on the scene before he left it, " Had there been such a school as this when I was a boy, I had not been a thief."

It was not, however, there, but in another school, that the circumstances happened which were mentioned to me, and formed, I thought, a warning to us against gathering all at once a large number of these neglected and undisciplined children. A school had been opened in another and very wild and wicked part of London. A considerable number of boys had been gathered in. The teacher ordered them, if I remember aright, to produce the books with which they had previously been furnished. Each of them put his hand into his pocket, but, instead of a book, produced a tobacco-pipe. He remonstrated: they answered him with clouds of smoke; and the upshot was a row and a riot, and the

master, over-mastered, was glad to escape with life and limb.
Such an issue was not to be risked here, and so we began with
a small number, and were gradually filling up, when symptoms
of that controversy began to appear which has now ended in an
open rupture.

In one newspaper of this city, it was asserted by an anony-
mous writer, that Roman Catholics were excluded from our
School. Our Committee was most unwilling to waste on controversy the time and attention which might be better employed,
and we neither took in sail, nor shifted our course, nor stayed one
moment, to answer these random shots ; but as people are ready
enough to suppose that what is not answered is unanswerable,
the Committee at length found it necessary to give this reckless
assertion the answer which it admitted and deserved,—a distinct
denial,—it being the fact, that at the very time that charge
was made, one half of the children were the children of nomi-
nally Roman Catholic parents. Obliged to abandon this position, the ground of attack was shifted ; and now it was asserted
that we were violating the Constitution of the Society, and conducting the Schools so as virtually to exclude Roman Catholic
children. In defence of themselves, and in answer to the accusations brought against them, of introducing " a system of religious tests into the Schools, and of excluding, in Roman Catholic children, the largest portion of those children for whom the
Schools were designed," the Acting Committee were led to publish
a " Statement," which, along with a " Minute of the General
Committee, approving of that Statement, will be found in the
Appendix to this " Supplement." Though the efforts of the
Committee were successful in satisfying a large portion of the
public that there was no foundation for the charges which had
been brought against us, there still remained some of our origi-
nal subscribers, between whom and the Committee there was an
important, and, as it proved to be, an irreconcileable difference.
These gentlemen requested the Lord Provost to call a meeting,
for the purpose of having " it clearly ascertained whether the
Schools will be conducted on a system which must necessarily

exclude children of the Roman Catholic, or any faith which differs from that of Protestant teachers." It was now feared, though not openly proclaimed, that an attempt would be made to exclude the Word of God from the Ragged School, and limit the education to secular instruction, leaving the Protestant and Roman Catholic parties to manage the religious interests of the children as they best might. The question, whether the Committee had honestly and fairly acted on the regulations approved of at the first public meeting, now sunk into comparative insignificance : it was swallowed up in the larger and far more important question, "Shall the candle of Divine truth shine in these Schools, or not ?" "Shall God's saving Word be taught to these unhappy outcasts, or not ?" The battle which had begun in Aberdeen and Dundee, had now extended to the capital; and the public meeting which had been called by the Lord Provost was, more than any meeting which had been for a long time held in Edinburgh, looked forward to with the liveliest interest by the warmest friends of Bible truth, and the wisest friends of these unhappy children. An attempt was made by some parties to represent the Committee as the enemies of religious toleration. Large bills covered the walls of our city, and called the friends of toleration to rally in the Music Hall, to counteract our sectarian proceedings. This attempt met with a failure as signal as it deserved. The Music Hall was crowded, but not with the parties whom this bill was meant to call out,—whether they were ashamed of it or not, we do not know,—but, with the exception of a very small portion of the audience, that large and influential assembly, embracing Episcopalians, Presbyterians, and Independents, unequivocally and strongly expressed its approval of all the steps which the Committee had taken, and of the resolution to which they had determined to adhere, that the Bible should be taught in these Schools during the ordinary school hours, and that religion should form an essential part of the education of these neglected children. We venture to say, that Edinburgh never uttered its voice more distinctly or more decidedly on any question, or on any occasion ; and as for ourselves, we can say, that we never went to a meeting with so much anxiety, nor left one with so much thankfulness. It was a blessed sight to see Protestants of all Evangelical denominations, and those of them who but a few years before had been arrayed against each other in the Voluntary and Non-Intrusion controversies, now fighting, side by side, around the Bible standard, with the kindness of brethren, and the keenness of men in earnest. A full report of that discussion has been published in a separate pamphlet,* and to that, for a full exposition of the views of the Managers of this Ragged School, we refer the reader of this " Supplement."

But for the publication of this pamphlet, we would have availed ourselves of this tenth edition to have entered at large on this important and vital question. In the hope, however, that the reader will examine that discussion for himself, and weigh the matter when he has thus heard both sides of the question, we forbear entering into its merits, further than to say, that we would tamper with no man's conscience, holding it to be the very principle of Protestantism that every man should be free to judge in matters of religion, uninfluenced either by fear or favour; and that to bribe a person to abandon his faith through the bread of a Ragged School, is nearly as bad as it would be to revive the fires and tortures of the Inquisition. We abhor the use of all such means; but we as much abhor the claim which any man makes to limit the free, the full, the unrestricted use of God's revealed Word. Imaged by the sun of heaven, which shines and sheds its heat on all, the Bible is common to all, needed by all, and the right of all; and that man violates as much my spiritual rights, who stands between me and the Word of God, as he does my natural, who stands between me and the light of day; and certainly, the greatest favour which the Roman Catholic priests could confer on those to whom they offer their services, would be to do for them what the philosopher in his tub requested might be done for him by

---

* "Report of a Discussion regarding Ragged Schools; held in the Music Hall, Edinburgh, on Friday, July 2, 1847." John Elder, 139, Prince's Street,

Alexander the Great, when the king asked how he could serve him :—" Stand out," said Diogenes, " between me and the sun." The ground we take up may be stated in a single sentence. Considering the condition of the children, and the character of the parents, who are living without the fear either of God or man, and who do not even make a profession of religion, the principles which might rule a national system of education do not apply here. Here the question cannot even be entertained, whether the religious tuition might not be safely left to the parents. Those for whom these Schools are established are untaught, uncared for, helpless outcasts ; and the state of their parents may, perhaps, be best illustrated by this single fact. In a mixed population of nominal Roman Catholics and Protestants, out of the first two hundred and fifty individuals in the Old Grayfriars' parish whom we visited on first coming to Edinburgh, there were not more than five who ever darkened the door of Christian church or chapel. To the children of such families, therefore, which are to all intents and purposes heathen families, we consider ourselves bound to act as if they were heathen children; and that one of the first things we have to do,—the best for their wellbeing in this life as well as the life to come,—is to teach them the way of salvation through the Word of God. Their souls, not less than their bodies, are cast upon our care ; and in such a case we cannot, we dare not, plead the excuse of Cain,—" Am I my brother's keeper ?" If, however, it should happen that some decent Roman Catholic parents found it necessary to seek for their children the benefit of a Ragged School, the Committee, as will be seen from one of their regulations, were willing to commit these children to the parents' charge upon the Sabbath day. Beyond this they could not go. They could not be parties in yielding to any Roman Catholic priest the right of withholding from any child of Adam the Word of God. In some respects we very much regret the differences that have arisen : they have separated us from some gentlemen who have treated us with the greatest kindness, and whose humanity and benevolence we hold in unfeigned admiration ; and, without any attempt to exclude the Bible from the common Ragged Schools, had it been proposed to set up a school of purely secular instruction, on the ground that there were a number of conscientious Roman Catholics who needed for their children a Ragged School, but who so bowed to the claims of the priesthood as to find the Bible a barrier in their way, we would have found no fault with the parties making such a proposal, nor felt ourselves in any way called to resist it. But that was not the proposition : it was one which, by the exclusion of the Bible from all our Schools, would have given them a Popish character, and one which we therefore felt ourselves bound to resist. It is a matter of thankfulness to find, that in the resolution which we have adopted, and the position which we have taken up, we have met with so much Christian sympathy ; and I cannot afford a better example of this, nor, perhaps, more effectively close this Supplement, than by submitting to the public the following letter, which I had the honour to receive from the Duke of Argyll :—

"Roseneath, July 8th.

" REV. SIR,

"I beg to be allowed to have my name placed on the list of Subscribers to the Ragged School which you have had such a principal share in founding, and the management of which, as regards the subject of religious instruction, you have so ably, and, I think, so triumphantly defended.

" I must apologise for the smallness of a contribution which, but for the urgent claims of a large and necessitous population, would have been somewhat more commensurate with my sense of the value and importance of the object.

" I cannot allow this opportunity to pass without expressing my humble but entire approval of the course which the Committee has pursued on the point above referred to. Between all those bodies which are commonly included under the term Protestant communions, there is so large a common ground, that there ought to be no difficulty whatever in teaching effectively, and with purpose, yet without sectarian bias, the doctrines and precepts of Christian truth. But the differences between them and the Roman Church are so numerous, pervading, and important, that the teaching which avoids them all must, I think, be formal, vague, and pointless. The nearest approach to anything which can be called religious teaching, compatible with such a system, is probably that contemplated by the Irish national scheme, in which readings are selected from the Bible. This has been supported by many excellent and able men. Not having any abstract objection, as some have, to the principle of selections, but thinking that everything depends on how large and ample such selections are, I should be sorry to say a word against a scheme which may be the best, or the only one possible in the peculiar circumstances of that country. But certainly I hold that such a scheme, as applied to the 'ragged' children of our great towns, would sacrifice a very large amount of positive and practical good, for the attainment of very small and very doubtful benefits. Where it can be reasonably expected that children, in addition to such (comparatively meagre) readings, will receive more positive instruction from parents, or guardians, or others interested in their welfare, the plan may not in itself be objectionable : Protestants will then not lose by the omissions,— Romanists may be allowed their benefit. But where no such expectation can reasonably be formed, the Protestants *must* lose much, and may lose all that is positive in religion ; whilst the Romanists will be in danger of being bound to their own communion only by its grosser ties,—by its observances, its priesthood, or its absolutions,—and lose all those deeper influences which have raised, and doubtless are raising, in the Roman Church, as earnest, as devoted, and as spiritually-minded Christians as the best who have believed in purer creeds.

"On these grounds, as well as on others which I cannot now refer to, I conceive such a plan to be essentially bad as applied to Ragged Schools; and as the Committee seems to me to have been unjustly assailed, I think it the duty of those who approve of your course in this respect to come forward now in its support.

"I am,

"Rev. Sir,

"Yours faithfully,

"ARGYLL.

"The Rev. Thomas Guthrie."

CONSTITUTION AND RULES

OF THE

ASSOCIATION FOR THE ESTABLISHMENT OF RAGGED INDUSTRIAL SCHOOLS FOR DESTITUTE CHILDREN IN EDINBURGH.

----

1. It is the object of this Association to reclaim the neglected and destitute children of Edinburgh, by affording them the benefits of a good common and Christian Education, and by training them to habits of regular industry, so as to enable them to earn an honest livelihood, and fit them for the duties of life.

2. With this view the Association shall establish and maintain one or more schools for such children, in such parts of the city or suburbs as may be found most advisable.

3. The following classes of children shall be excluded :—1st, Those who are already regularly attending Day-Schools ;—2d, Those whose parents are earning a regular income, and able to procure education for their children ;—3d, Those who are receiving, or entitled to receive, support and education from the Parochial Boards ;—with this declaration, that it shall be in the power of the Acting Committee to deal with special cases, although falling under any of these classes, having regard always to the special objects of the Association.

4. The Association shall consist of all Subscribers of Ten Shillings per annum and upwards, and of all Donors of Five Pounds and upwards.

5. It shall be governed by a General Committee, consisting of fifty Members (fifteen being a quorum), and an Acting Committee, consisting of twenty-five Members (five being a quorum), with a Secretary and Treasurer. The Acting Committee shall be entitled to be present and vote at all Meetings of the General Committee.

6. A Meeting of the Association shall be held annually, in April, when a Report of the proceedings shall be read, and the Committees and Office-Bearers elected for the ensuing year. The Acting Committee shall meet at least once every month.

7. The Acting Committee shall have power to elect the Office-Bearers, to appoint Local Committees, and to make laws and regulations to be observed in conducting the business of the Association ; and all Schools to be established by the Association shall be subject to such laws and regulations ; but no school shall be established without the consent of the General Committee.

8. The appointment of Teachers, and other officers, shall be made by the Acting Committee.

9. The general plan upon which the Schools shall be conducted shall be as follows, viz. :—

To give the children an allowance of food for their daily support.

To instruct them in reading, writing, and arithmetic.

To train them in habits of industry, by instructing and employing them daily in such sorts of work as are suited to their years.

To teach them the truths of the gospel, making the Holy Scriptures the groundwork of instruction.

On Sabbath the children shall receive food as on other days, and such religious instruction as shall be arranged by the Acting Committee.

STATEMENT

BY THE

ACTING COMMITTEE OF THE ASSOCIATION FOR ESTABLISHING RAGGED OR INDUSTRIAL SCHOOLS.

THE Committee having had their attention called to certain articles and letters in a respectable newspaper in this city, of a nature fitted to cause misconception and distrust in the mind of the public on the subject of religious teaching in their schools, think it necessary to publish the following statement :—

By the Constitution and Rules of the Association it is declared, that " It is the object of this Association to reclaim the neglected or profligate children of Edinburgh, by affording them the benefits of a good common and Christian education, and by training them to habits of regular industry, so as to enable them to earn an honest livelihood, and fit them for the duties of life ;" and, in regard to the general plan upon which the schools are to be conducted, it is declared that the children shall be taught " the truths of the gospel, making the Holy Scriptures the groundwork of instruction ;" and that " on Sabbath the children shall receive food as on other days, and such religious instruction as shall be arranged by the Acting Committee."

The Constitution and Rules, from which these quotations are taken, were fully discussed at a large meeting, in the Council Chambers, of the Preliminary Committee appointed by the Lord Provost, and approved of by them. They were thereafter submitted to the public meeting in the Music Hall, and received the unanimous approval of that meeting ; and the general plan of the schools has been kept prominently in the view of the public in all the statements and appeals issued by the Committee with a view to obtaining contributions for the schools.   From the large amount of subscriptions that have already been received, the Committee are happy to think that the principles of the Association have met with the general confidence of the public.

These principles have been, and will continue to be, faithfully adhered to in the management of the schools.   The religious instruction conveyed at these schools must necessarily be of the most simple and elementary kind, so as to be adapted to the tender years and gross ignorance of the children.   Its entire freedom from all sectarian bias is effectually secured by the superintendence of a Committee impartially selected from the various leading religious bodies composing the great bulk of the community. The only books hitherto used in the school have been the Bible and the First and Second Books of Education, published under the superintendence of the Commissioners of National Education in Ireland.   The Committee feel that they cannot hope for a blessing on their schools if religion is not the pervading principle of the instruction given to the children.

The instruction on the Lord's day is conducted on like principles as on week-days, though, of course, it bears a more purely religious character. In order to meet the case of those parents who may have conscientious objections to their children receiving the more special religious instruction communicated on Sabbath, or attending public worship with the teacher, provision is made that such parents, provided they are in a condition to be entrusted with the care of their children, shall be allowed to withdraw them for the purpose of attending their own place of worship, of whatever denomination.

The Committee feel assured that this explanatory statement will be sufficient to satisfy the public that the accusations brought against them, of introducing a "system of religious tests" into the schools, and of "excluding the largest portion of those children for whom the schools were designed," are entirely without foundation.

It must be obvious that an institution of this kind, intended to provide a home, food, moral and industrial training, as well as the ordinary branches of scholarship, for children otherwise utterly destitute of all these, is by no means on the same footing with ordinary day schools, in which applicants may select the branches they may wish to attend; and cannot, therefore, be judged of on the same principles. The Committee view themselves as not in the position of mere ordinary instructors, but as coming, in the great majority of cases, in the place of parents, with regard to the temporal as well as spiritual interests of the children. As parents, they cannot throw off the responsibility attaching to them of enlightening the minds of the children; and, in so doing, they cannot but give them that instruction which is best calculated to reclaim the children from the miserable condition in which they are found. It would be utterly ruinous to the plan, and defeat all its benevolent purposes, especially considering the criminal and vagrant habits of the children who are to be benefited by it, if any other system were adopted than that of subjecting them all to the entire moral and religious discipline,—simply based upon the Word of God,—which it purposes to bring to bear upon them.

It may be added, that although it has been alleged that those principles of this Association which are now attacked are peculiar to it, the Committee do not know of any institution of the kind now in existence in Scotland which is not founded upon the very same principles.

The Committee conclude with expressing their unanimous and earnest desire to follow out thoroughly the sound principles on which the Association is founded. They ask to be judged by what they are now doing; and to be believed when they state, in the strongest manner, their anxious wish to avoid sectarianism, and to pursue their work earnestly and cheerfully in the spirit of their Divine Master, who went about doing good. They request the public to visit the schools, and to judge for themselves whether they are efficiently and properly conducted.

By appointment of the Acting Committee,

AND. JAMESON, *Convener.*

Edinburgh, 14th June 1847.

At a Meeting of the General Committee of the Association for Establishing Ragged or Industrial Schools in Edinburgh, held in No. 6, York Place, on 18th June 1847,

The LORD PROVOST in the Chair,

The following Resolutions were moved by JAMES CRAUFURD, Esq. Advocate, seconded by Dr W. P. ALISON, and agreed to :—

That this meeting approve of the " Statement of the Acting Committee ;" but since it appears that some misapprehension prevails in regard to the principles on which the schools are conducted,

Resolved,

1st, That the General Committee emphatically disclaim all intention of using the advantages held out by these schools as a means of tempting Roman Catholics to the abandonment or compromise of opinions which they conscientiously entertain. The reclaiming of children from ignorance and crime, not their conversion from Romanism, is the aim of the Committee and the object of the schools ; and the Committee rejoice to know that, both in Aberdeen, and hitherto in Edinburgh, the children of Roman Catholic parents have attended the schools without any objection being made.

2d, That no catechism, or other formula of doctrine, is or shall be taught to any child whose parents object to it.

3d, That children are and shall be excused from attendance at school, or at worship, on the Sabbath day, whose parents object to their attendance, and undertake that the children are otherwise religiously instructed, according to the tenets of the communion to which they belong, provided they are in a condition to be entrusted with the care of their children.

EDINBURGH : PRINTED BY MILLER AND FAIRLY.

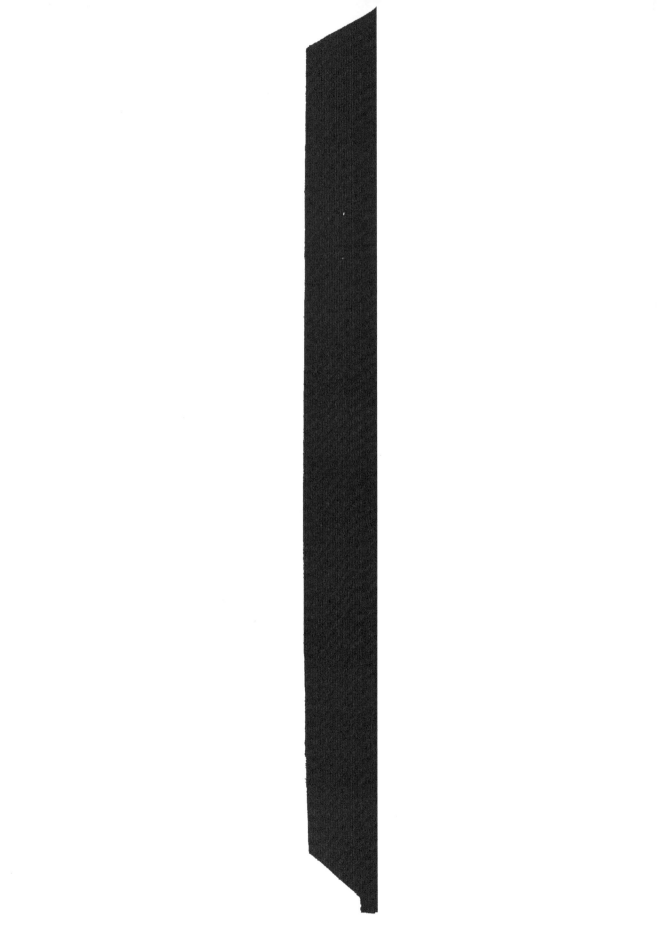

CPSIA information can be obtained at www.ICGtesting.com
Printed in the USA
LVOW03s2014161014

409097LV00013B/546/P